Shoes by Twos

Lalie Harcourt & Ricki Wortzman

Illustrated by Tina Holdcroft

Dominie Press, Inc.

Shoes, shoes,
come in twos.

Here is Sheila.
She sells shoes.

She sells shoes
to match all kinds of clothes.

Here is Kiri. She loves to clap and spin.
Which shoes will she choose?

tap!
tap!

Shoes, shoes,
come in twos.
There are 2!
There are 2 shoes spinning.
Tap, tap!

6

Here is Matt. He loves to march and shout.
Which shoes will he choose?

Shoes, shoes,
come in twos.
There are 2, 4!
There are 4 shoes marching.
Tap, tap! Clomp, clomp!

Here is Jack. He loves to laugh and jump.
Which shoes will he choose?

Shoes, shoes,
come in twos.
There are 2, 4, 6!
There are 6 shoes jumping.
Tap, tap! Clomp, clomp!
Squeak, squeak!

Here is Don. He loves
to whistle and dance.
Which shoes will he choose?

Shoes, shoes,
come in twos.
There are 2, 4, 6, 8!
There are 8 shoes dancing.
Tap, tap! Clomp, clomp!
Squeak, squeak! Squish, squish!

Here is Lucy. She loves to sing and leap.
Which shoes will she choose?

Shoes, shoes,
come in twos.
There are 2, 4, 6, 8, 10!
There are 10 shoes leaping.
Tap, tap! Clomp, clomp!
Squeak, squeak! Squish, squish!
Flip-flop, flip-flop!

"I sold a lot of shoes today!"

"Shoes, shoes,
I wonder what else comes in twos."